GREATER AKRON MEMORIES

A PICTORIAL HISTORY OF THE 1800s THROUGH THE 1930s

Akron Beacon Journal/Ohio.com

Multimedia Company

On the cover:

Market and Main Streets, circa 1916.
COURTESY SUMMIT COUNTY HISTORICAL SOCIETY, CARL H. POCKRANDT COLLECTION

ACKNOWLEDGMENTS

The following organizations have contributed greatly to this project:

*The Summit County Historical Society of Akron, OH
Akron-Summit County Public Library*

Photos curated by Brooke Horn and Brad Fenison.

Published by Pediment Publishing, a division of The Pediment Group, Inc.
www.pediment.com • Printed in Canada.

FOREWORD

The longer you look at an old photograph, the more you see. And the more you see, the further you travel. The clock ticks backward, the decades melt away, and a century reverses in the blink of an eye.

Greater Akron Memories: A Pictorial History of the 1800s Through the 1930s opens a portal to a world that no longer exists, but looks uncannily familiar. Cultivated from the archives of the Akron-Summit County Public Library, The Summit County Historical Society of Akron, OH, and the *Akron Beacon Journal/Ohio.com*, this commemorative book features hundreds of stunning, historical photographs, including many rare, unusual, and never-before-published images.

Each photograph tells a story. Look carefully at the people who are pictured. Note the expressions on their faces, the pride and determination in their eyes. Observe their snazzy suits, fancy dresses, and jaunty hats. Meet your ancestors. These are the sturdy generations who cemented Greater Akron's place in history.

The street names may be recognizable, but many of the famous landmarks are distant memories today. We can only revisit these magnificent buildings and ornate architecture in pictures.

Greater Akron Memories examines the profound and the mundane. It captures the community at work and at play, revealing quiet moments and extravagant spectacles, recalling the triumphs and tragedies of an industrial city on the move.

And it does so in glorious, luminous, black and white photographs.

You will want to savor every detail of every moment pictured in this book. Start at the beginning and work your way forward, and when you reach the final page, flip back and start again. You will find things that you missed the first time around.

Ready? Let's travel back in time.

Mark J. Price
Akron Beacon Journal/Ohio.com
September 17, 2018

TABLE OF CONTENTS

OPPOSITE: Knights Templar Parade at South Howard and Main Streets, 1916. COURTESY SUMMIT COUNTY HISTORICAL SOCIETY, CARL H. POCKRANDT COLLECTION

chapter one

VIEWS AND STREET SCENES

OPPOSITE: View of Akron including the Goodyear Tire & Rubber Company and East Market Street, circa 1930.

COURTESY SUMMIT COUNTY HISTORICAL SOCIETY, CARL H. POCKRANDT COLLECTION

ABOVE: The Pennsylvania and Ohio Canal at South Main Street from the rear of Howard Street, 1870. The dwelling and yard in the foreground later became the site of the O'Neil and Dyas store. The canal ran from Akron across the Ravenna Summit, down the Cuyahoga and Mahoning Rivers, and connected with the Beaver and Erie Canal just south of New Castle, Pennsylvania. It had a rise of 424 feet and required 54 locks, two aqueducts, nine dams and 57 road bridges. Construction began in 1835 and took five years to complete. Industrial expansion and development of the railroad led to its official closure in 1877.
COURTESY AKRON-SUMMIT COUNTY PUBLIC LIBRARY, SAMUEL LANE COLLECTION

RIGHT: Market and Howard Streets, circa 1858. The building in the distance is the Etna Mill. On the corner is the store opened by Philander D. Hall in 1835. The area served as Akron's central business district for a time and was known as Hall's Corners for nearly 100 years.
COURTESY SUMMIT COUNTY HISTORICAL SOCIETY

LEFT: View of Akron, 1878. Included are Jumbo Mills, Buchtel College, First Church of Christ, the German Lutheran Church, First Methodist Episcopal Church, Fire Station No. 1, Courthouse, Masonic Building, George Dale's Store, and Hower Mill.
COURTESY SUMMIT COUNTY HISTORICAL SOCIETY, BUILDING SUMMIT COUNTY COLLECTION

BELOW LEFT: South Howard Street looking south from Market Street, circa 1890.
COURTESY SUMMIT COUNTY HISTORICAL SOCIETY, CARL H. POCKRANDT COLLECTION

BELOW: Looking east at Center Street from Broadway, circa 1889.
COURTESY SUMMIT COUNTY HISTORICAL SOCIETY

ABOVE Panoramic view of Akron, circa 1911.
COURTESY LIBRARY OF CONGRESS / #LC-USZ62-122221

OPPOSITE BOTTOM LEFT: West side of
Main Street looking north, circa 1910.
COURTESY SUMMIT COUNTY HISTORICAL SOCIETY, CARL H. POCKRANDT COLLECTION

LEFT: Market Street looking east from Canal Street in
downtown, 1904. The Carnegie Library is in the distance
on the left.
COURTESY AKRON-SUMMIT COUNTY PUBLIC LIBRARY, GENERAL PHOTOGRAPH COLLECTION

LEFT: Market and Main Streets, circa 1916.
COURTESY SUMMIT COUNTY HISTORICAL SOCIETY, CARL H. POCKRANDT COLLECTION

OPPOSITE: View of Main Street, circa 1916.
COURTESY SUMMIT COUNTY HISTORICAL SOCIETY, CARL H. POCKRANDT COLLECTION

BELOW LEFT: Main Street at the Flatiron Building, circa 1914.
COURTESY SUMMIT COUNTY HISTORICAL SOCIETY, CARL H. POCKRANDT COLLECTION

BELOW: Looking north on Howard Street during rebuilding of Cuyahoga River Bridge, circa 1914.
COURTESY SUMMIT COUNTY HISTORICAL SOCIETY, CARL H. POCKRANDT COLLECTION

LEFT: View of the North Hill Viaduct, circa 1920. It was the first direct connection across the Little Cuyahoga River valley in Akron. The North Hill Viaduct connected Main Street to North Hill. The viaduct was demolished in 1978 and replaced by the All-America Bridge (Y-Bridge).
COURTESY SUMMIT COUNTY HISTORICAL SOCIETY, BUILDING SUMMIT COUNTY COLLECTION

OPPOSITE: Main Street at Mill Street, 1920s.
COURTESY SUMMIT COUNTY HISTORICAL SOCIETY, CARL H. POCKRANDT COLLECTION

BELOW LEFT: Looking east at the Armory in downtown Akron, 1920s. The Armory was completed in 1918 and was the largest indoor gathering place in the city for many years. While the main function of the Armory was to be a training site for the local National Guard, its auditorium was used for many civic and entertainment purposes. The Armory was demolished in 1982 to make way for the Ocasek Office Building. COURTESY AKRON BEACON JOURNAL

BELOW: View of the YMCA in downtown Akron, circa 1920.
COURTESY AKRON-SUMMIT COUNTY PUBLIC LIBRARY, SHORTY FULTON COLLECTION

RIGHT: Aerial view of the USS *Akron* over the Goodyear Tire & Rubber Company, circa 1930. COURTESY AKRON-SUMMIT COUNTY PUBLIC LIBRARY, SHORTY FULTON COLLECTION

BELOW RIGHT: High Level Bridge over the Cuyahoga River connecting Akron to Cuyahoga Falls, circa 1929. The bridge opened in 1915 and was demolished in 1950, after a new bridge was built in 1949. COURTESY AKRON BEACON JOURNAL

BELOW: The USS *Akron* flying over the Goodyear Tire & Rubber Company, 1931. COURTESY AKRON-SUMMIT COUNTY PUBLIC LIBRARY, GENERAL PHOTOGRAPH COLLECTION

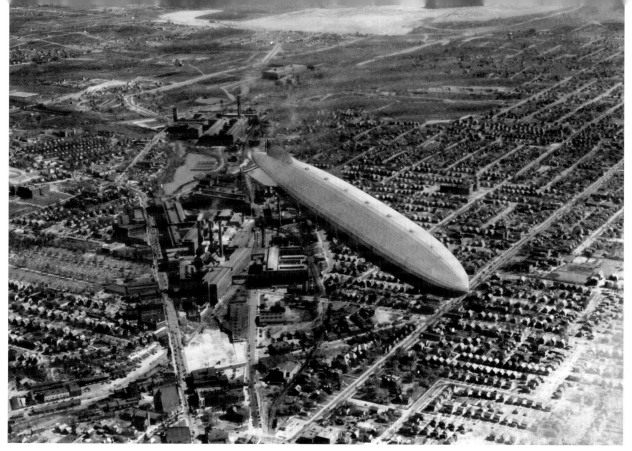

LEFT: North Hill Viaduct, 1930s. COURTESY AKRON BEACON JOURNAL

BELOW: Front Street in Cuyahoga Falls, circa 1938. COURTESY SUMMIT COUNTY HISTORICAL SOCIETY, CARL H. POCKRANDT COLLECTION

chapter two

COMMERCE

OPPOSITE: Loomis Hardware Store in Cuyahoga Falls, circa 1895. COURTESY SUMMIT COUNTY HISTORICAL SOCIETY

RIGHT: John Wolf dry goods store at the corner of Market and Main Streets, circa 1889.
COURTESY SUMMIT COUNTY HISTORICAL SOCIETY, CARL H. POCKRANDT COLLECTION

BELOW RIGHT: Randall L. McAllister, proprietor, standing in the doorway of his Louisville Liquor Store at 188 South Howard Street, circa 1889.
COURTESY SUMMIT COUNTY HISTORICAL SOCIETY

BELOW: Wilhelm and Brodt Meat Market near Main and Exchange Streets, circa 1890.
COURTESY SUMMIT COUNTY HISTORICAL SOCIETY, CARL H. POCKRANDT COLLECTION

ABOVE: Diefendorff's Little Jersey Dairy, an early Akron milk peddler, circa 1890. COURTESY SUMMIT COUNTY HISTORICAL SOCIETY, CARL H. POCKRANDT COLLECTION

LEFT: Employees of the Werner Printing and Lithographing Company, circa 1890. COURTESY SUMMIT COUNTY HISTORICAL SOCIETY

ABOVE: Business office in Akron, circa 1895. COURTESY AKRON BEACON JOURNAL

ABOVE RIGHT: Group of women attending an outing of the bindery and wrapping department of the Werner Printing Company at Silver Lake, circa 1900. COURTESY AKRON BEACON JOURNAL

RIGHT: Wise Furnace Company employees, circa 1900.
COURTESY SUMMIT COUNTY HISTORICAL SOCIETY, BUILDING SUMMIT COUNTY COLLECTION

ABOVE: Bar at Charles Schroeder's Buckeye Cafe, 168 East Center Street in Akron, circa 1910. COURTESY AKRON BEACON JOURNAL

ABOVE LEFT: Dollar Savings Bank in Akron, May 28, 1904. Included in the photo are: Dr. L. E. Sisler, Fred A. Boron, Benjamin M. J. Welday, Alice E. McAllister. COURTESY SUMMIT COUNTY HISTORICAL SOCIETY

LEFT: Newsboys with their supervisor before hawking their product on the streets of Akron, circa 1910. COURTESY AKRON BEACON JOURNAL

ABOVE: "Going Out of Business Sale" at Knofler's clothing store in the Abbey building on Main Street, April 1914. The M. O'Neil Company bought the building next to it, which was later torn down to make way for a new building that housed the S. S. Kresge Company. COURTESY SUMMIT COUNTY HISTORICAL SOCIETY

OPPOSITE: Central Office Building on Main and Mill Streets, circa 1917. COURTESY SUMMIT COUNTY HISTORICAL SOCIETY, CARL H. POCKRANDT COLLECTION

RIGHT: Prospect Buick Co. on Prospect Street between East Mill and East Market Streets, circa 1916. COURTESY SUMMIT COUNTY HISTORICAL SOCIETY

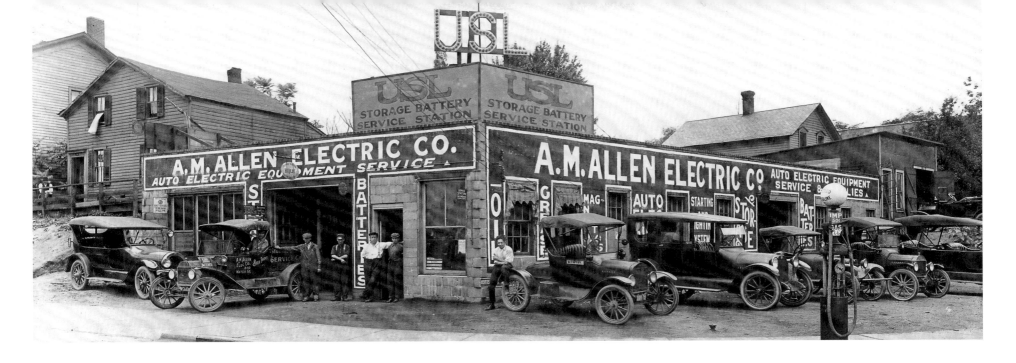

ABOVE: A. M. Allen Electric Co. at the corner of West Buchtel Avenue and Water Street in Akron, circa 1925. COURTESY SUMMIT COUNTY HISTORICAL SOCIETY, BUILDING SUMMIT COUNTY COLLECTION

OPPOSITE: State Bank on Market and Main Streets, circa 1917. COURTESY SUMMIT COUNTY HISTORICAL SOCIETY, CARL H. POCKRANDT COLLECTION

LEFT: *Akron Beacon Journal* editorial room on East Market Street, circa 1929. COURTESY AKRON BEACON JOURNAL

RIGHT: Federman's Department Store at the corner of South Main and Mill Streets, circa 1930. COURTESY SUMMIT COUNTY HISTORICAL SOCIETY

OPPOSITE TOP: The Canteen restaurant at 1612 State Road in Cuyahoga Falls, circa 1933. COURTESY SUMMIT COUNTY HISTORICAL SOCIETY

OPPOSITE BOTTOM RIGHT: Tailor Louis Aiuto (left) in his tailor shop at 249 North Howard Street in Akron, circa 1930. He worked out of the Howard Street location for 47 years. COURTESY AKRON-SUMMIT COUNTY PUBLIC LIBRARY, GENERAL PHOTOGRAPH COLLECTION

OPPOSITE BOTTOM LEFT: *Beacon Journal* employees, 1930s. COURTESY AKRON BEACON JOURNAL

BELOW: The Post Brothers Market on the southwest corner of Wilbeth and Manchester Roads in Kenmore, circa 1930. Founded in 1908, the village of Kenmore was built along the streetcar lines between Akron and Barberton. COURTESY AKRON-SUMMIT COUNTY PUBLIC LIBRARY, GENERAL PHOTOGRAPH COLLECTION

chapter three

INDUSTRY

OPPOSITE: Men working on the skeleton of the USS *Akron* in 1929. The USS *Akron* (ZRS-4) was a helium-filled, rigid airship of the US Navy that was destroyed in a thunderstorm off the coast of New Jersey on the morning of April 4, 1933, killing 73 of the 76 crewmen and passengers. Construction of ZRS-4 began on October 31, 1929, at the Goodyear Airdock in Springfield Township by the Goodyear-Zeppelin Corporation. Because it was the largest airship to be built in America at the time, a special hangar was constructed and a team of experienced German airship engineers, led by Chief Designer Karl Arnstein, instructed and supported design and construction of both US Navy airships USS *Akron* and USS *Macon*.
COURTESY AKRON BEACON JOURNAL

RIGHT: Burkhardt Brewery, circa 1879. It was built on Sherman Street near Grant Street by William Burkhardt in 1874. After William died in 1882, his wife, Margaretha, and later on his sons, William and Gustav, continued to successfully run the business. The man in the white apron, standing in front, is William. Next to him is his partner Fritz Gaessler.

BELOW RIGHT: Goodrich factory workers, circa 1890.

BELOW: Schumacher "Jumbo Mills" on Summit Street, circa 1880. It burned in March 1886.

LEFT: Akron Iron Works employees, circa 1890. The company was organized in 1866 and operated until the plant burned in 1897. While the company did reorganize in 1900, it did not rebuild or resume operations. COURTESY SUMMIT COUNTY HISTORICAL SOCIETY

BELOW LEFT: Burkhardt Brewery, circa 1900. COURTESY SUMMIT COUNTY HISTORICAL SOCIETY, CARL H. POCKRANDT COLLECTION

BELOW: Six workers at Kubler Match Factory taking a break, circa 1900. COURTESY SUMMIT COUNTY HISTORICAL SOCIETY, BUILDING SUMMIT COUNTY COLLECTION

ABOVE: Colonial Salt Company on Manchester Road in Kenmore, circa 1903.
COURTESY SUMMIT COUNTY HISTORICAL SOCIETY

OPPOSITE TOP: Employees at the Diamond Rubber Company at 478-534 South Main, circa 1907. O. C. Barber, president of the Diamond Match Company and founder of the city of Barberton, established the Diamond Rubber Company in 1894 under the name the Sherbondy Rubber Company. In 1896, the name was changed to the Diamond Rubber Company when it began the manufacture of automobile tires. The Diamond Rubber Company was eventually merged with B. F. Goodrich in 1912. COURTESY AKRON BEACON JOURNAL

OPPOSITE BOTTOM RIGHT: All-female crew working for Firestone Tire & Rubber Company in Akron, 1910. COURTESY AKRON-SUMMIT COUNTY PUBLIC LIBRARY, GENERAL PHOTOGRAPH COLLECTION

OPPOSITE BOTTOM LEFT: Female employees of the B. F. Goodrich box factory, circa 1907. Some of them dressed up as men and all are in costume for a party. Back row, from left: Margaret Schellin, Maud Diemer, Anna Huggler, Theresa Bissonett, Kate Meier, Mary Tillett, Lillian Herman, Lillian Dressler. Front row: Crystal Dressler, Bertha Hupfer. COURTESY AKRON BEACON JOURNAL

RIGHT: The heater room at the Cleveland-Akron Bag Company on Boston Mills Road, Boston Township, circa 1910. COURTESY AKRON BEACON JOURNAL

ABOVE RIGHT: Early pilots and construction workers on the balloons and non-rigid airships produced by Goodyear, circa 1920. The men are standing in front of the RS-1, the only semi-rigid airship built by Goodyear. Identified are John Yingling (third from left), George Wiedner (fifth from left), V. L. Smith (eighth), Paul Segal (ninth), K.L. Fickes (10th), August O'Neill (11th), John Cooper (16th) and Jack Yolton (17th). COURTESY AKRON BEACON JOURNAL

OPPOSITE TOP: Crowds of people in the Goodyear Airdock for the ring-laying ceremony that marked the start of construction, of the USS *Akron,* November 9, 1929.
COURTESY SUMMIT COUNTY HISTORICAL SOCIETY, CARL H. POCKRANDT COLLECTION

OPPOSITE BOTTOM RIGHT: Workers for the Firestone Tire & Rubber Company on the assembly line, circa 1920. COURTESY AKRON-SUMMIT COUNTY PUBLIC LIBRARY, GENERAL PHOTOGRAPH COLLECTION

OPPOSITE BOTTOM LEFT: Laborer working with crude rubber from Brazil being cracked by the rubber-cracking machine at the Goodyear tire factory, 1928.
COURTESY LIBRARY OF CONGRESS / #LC-USZ62-113946

BELOW RIGHT: The Robinson Clay Product Company plant No. 9, circa 1910. The company operated nine plants. They made sewer pipe, fine brick, and stoneware.
COURTESY SUMMIT COUNTY HISTORICAL SOCIETY, BUILDING SUMMIT COUNTY COLLECTION

ABOVE: Goodyear airship pilots, circa 1930. Front row, from left: Sam Sheppard, R. L. Hobensack, James Stealey, Frank Trotter, Ray Roderick, Larry P. Furculow, William Hudson, Russell Crosier, Walter Massie, R. L. Wilson. Back row: J. A. Boettner, C. E. Brannigan, John Cooper, August O'Neill, V. L. Smith, Karl Lange, Roland Blair, Alexander Munro, H. W. Crum, K. L. Fickes. COURTESY AKRON BEACON JOURNAL

ABOVE RIGHT: Excavation at the *Akron Beacon Journal* building on East Market Street in Akron, November 1, 1929. COURTESY AKRON BEACON JOURNAL

OPPOSITE: Construction workers transporting dirt during the construction of the Akron Municipal Airport. COURTESY AKRON-SUMMIT COUNTY PUBLIC LIBRARY, SHORTY FULTON COLLECTION

RIGHT: The Goodyear Airdock under construction, May 17, 1929. The Goodyear Airdock in Akron was constructed by the Goodyear-Zeppelin Corporation from plans created by the Wilbur Watson Engineering Company of Cleveland. With the construction of the Airdock, Akron became one of the centers for development and construction of lighter-than-air ships. COURTESY AKRON BEACON JOURNAL

RIGHT: Construction of the nose of the USS *Akron*, 1931. COURTESY AKRON-SUMMIT COUNTY PUBLIC LIBRARY, GENERAL PHOTOGRAPH COLLECTION

OPPOSITE LEFT: Karl Arnstein (left) and two unidentified men standing on the testing block to observe one of the USS *Akron's* propellers, 1931. The propellers on the USS *Akron* could be tilted horizontal or vertical. COURTESY AKRON-SUMMIT COUNTY PUBLIC LIBRARY, GENERAL PHOTOGRAPH COLLECTION

OPPOSITE TOP RIGHT: Inside view of the frame of the USS *Akron*, 1931. COURTESY AKRON-SUMMIT COUNTY PUBLIC LIBRARY, GENERAL PHOTOGRAPH COLLECTION

OPPOSITE BOTTOM RIGHT: The USS *Akron* taking off at the Akron Municipal Airport, 1931. COURTESY AKRON-SUMMIT COUNTY PUBLIC LIBRARY, GENERAL PHOTOGRAPH COLLECTION

BELOW: The metal skeleton of the USS *Akron* being constructed for the Navy at the Goodyear-Zeppelin factory in hangar at Akron, 1930. COURTESY LIBRARY OF CONGRESS / # LC-USZ62-74685

LEFT: Electronics technician at Goodyear Aircraft Corporation in Akron, 1939. COURTESY LIBRARY OF CONGRESS / #LC-DIG-FSAC-1A35065

OPPOSITE: Workers taking synthetic rubber off the rolling mill at the B. F. Goodrich Company plant in Akron, 1939. Synthetic rubber made by the "Ameripol" process is derived from butadiene (a petroleum derivative). In this rolling mill, the crumbs of rubber are squeezed dry of excess water and pressed together into the blanket shown here. COURTESY LIBRARY OF CONGRESS / #LC-DIG-FSAC-1A35068

BELOW: Bricklayers working on a new building in Akron, March 24, 1938. In 1938, the city of Akron began a building inspection project that determined 100 buildings were in need of immediate repair and 105 more were in need of eventual repair. The project created an estimated 700 new jobs and repair estimates were around $200,000. The Hotel Anthony Wayne, which was located on South Main Street, can be seen in the background. COURTESY AKRON BEACON JOURNAL

chapter four

TRANSPORTATION

OPPOSITE: John R. Gammeter in his early flying machine on a fairway at Portage Country Club, early 1900s. Gammeter had a number of inventions including the first machine for winding golf balls with rubber thread. Gammeter, owner of Akron's first plane, is poised for takeoff from a fairway at Portage Country Club (the old clubhouse is in the background). We don't know how high he went, or how far, but he survived. Gammeter gained fame as an inventor and a total of 266 inventions were credited to him. COURTESY SUMMIT COUNTY HISTORICAL SOCIETY, BUILDING SUMMIT COUNTY COLLECTION

RIGHT: Akron's first electric streetcar (right) and its last horse-drawn car, October 3, 1888. COURTESY SUMMIT COUNTY HISTORICAL SOCIETY

OPPOSITE: Valley Railroad Passenger Station in Akron, late 1800s. It was built in 1888. COURTESY SUMMIT COUNTY HISTORICAL SOCIETY, BUILDING SUMMIT COUNTY COLLECTION

BELOW RIGHT: The steamboat, *Will Dailey*, from the shore of Silver Lake, circa 1890. William H. Dailey built the steamer in 1883 and it operated for 17 seasons without incident. It was destroyed by fire in June 1900 and the *Mayflower* replaced it. COURTESY AKRON BEACON JOURNAL

BELOW: Akron's first Union Depot, circa 1880. It was located on Mill Street opposite the intersection of Summit Street from 1852 until 1891. COURTESY SUMMIT COUNTY HISTORICAL SOCIETY, BUILDING SUMMIT COUNTY COLLECTION

RIGHT: Open streetcar and operators, circa 1900.
COURTESY SUMMIT COUNTY HISTORICAL SOCIETY

OPPOSITE: Streetcars crossing the Gorge High Level Bridge, circa 1900. COURTESY SUMMIT COUNTY HISTORICAL SOCIETY, CARL H. POCKRANDT COLLECTION

BELOW RIGHT: The ferry on the Cuyahoga River that ran between Akron and Cuyahoga Falls, circa 1900.
COURTESY SUMMIT COUNTY HISTORICAL SOCIETY, CARL H. POCKRANDT COLLECTION

BELOW: John and Margaret Walsh out for a drive with friends and family, 1906. COURTESY SUMMIT COUNTY HISTORICAL SOCIETY

ABOVE: Hawkins railroad station, circa 1908.
COURTESY SUMMIT COUNTY HISTORICAL SOCIETY, CARL H. POCKRANDT COLLECTION

ABOVE RIGHT: The steamboat, *Chautauquan*, which was the last steamboat built for Silver Lake Amusement Park in Akron, circa 1912. The boat was completed in 1910. When Silver Lake Park was sold in 1918, the *Chautauquan* was moved to Springfield Lake. COURTESY AKRON BEACON JOURNAL

OPPOSITE: Building the High Level Bridge between Akron and Cuyahoga Falls, circa 1914. Construction on the bridge began in 1913 and it opened in 1915.
COURTESY SUMMIT COUNTY HISTORICAL SOCIETY, CARL H. POCKRANDT COLLECTION

RIGHT: Peninsula railroad station, circa 1908.
COURTESY SUMMIT COUNTY HISTORICAL SOCIETY, CARL H. POCKRANDT COLLECTION

LEFT: Twin Coach No. 1378 picking up passengers on Main Street in downtown Akron, 1929. The coach was headed for Cuyahoga Falls. COURTESY AKRON METRO REGIONAL TRANSPORTATION AUTHORITY COLLECTION

OPPOSITE: Union Depot, circa 1918. COURTESY SUMMIT COUNTY HISTORICAL SOCIETY, CARL H. POCKRANDT COLLECTION

BELOW: B&O engine No. 5209 pulling cars loaded with passengers near the Goodyear Airdock in Akron, circa 1929. The Airdock was constructed in 1929 by the Goodyear-Zeppelin Corporation as the world's largest building without interior supports. It measured 1,175 feet long, 325 feet wide, and 211 feet high. COURTESY AKRON BEACON JOURNAL

LEFT: City Cab car and driver, early 1930s. COURTESY SUMMIT COUNTY HISTORICAL SOCIETY, BUILDING SUMMIT COUNTY COLLECTION

OPPOSITE TOP: Akron & Barberton Belt Railroad (A&BBRR) steam engine, circa 1930. The railroad was founded in 1902 by Ohio C. Barber, a prominent industrialist and owner of the Diamond Match Company in Barberton, Ohio. The belt line was sold by Barber and became a shared enterprise of several larger railroad corporations. At its peak, the A&BBRR operated more than 40 miles of track that connected numerous industries between Barberton and East Akron. COURTESY AKRON-SUMMIT COUNTY PUBLIC LIBRARY, GENERAL PHOTOGRAPH COLLECTION

OPPOSITE BOTTOM LEFT: Givens Trucking Company's fleet of trucks owned by William A. Givens, circa 1931. COURTESY AKRON-SUMMIT COUNTY PUBLIC LIBRARY, GENERAL PHOTOGRAPH COLLECTION

OPPOSITE BOTTOM RIGHT: Twin Coach No. 1363 on Main Street in downtown Akron, 1929. The Twin Coach was created by brothers William B. and Frank R. Fageol of Kent, Ohio. Twin Coaches had two engines which allowed for larger passenger loads. COURTESY AKRON METRO REGIONAL TRANSPORTATION AUTHORITY COLLECTION

BELOW LEFT: Joe Ennis and an unidentified man standing by a Motor Cargo Company truck, circa 1930. In 1930, Owen Orr and his father, James Orr, opened the Akron Motor Cargo Company. In 1939, the company name changed to Motor Cargo Inc. COURTESY AKRON-SUMMIT COUNTY PUBLIC LIBRARY, GENERAL PHOTOGRAPH COLLECTION

RIGHT: Men standing in front of a Mack Boxcar bus in Akron, circa 1934. This bus is one of nine Mack Model 6-CL-38 coaches purchased in 1934, series 1403-1411. COURTESY AKRON-SUMMIT COUNTY PUBLIC LIBRARY, AKRON METRO REGIONAL TRANSPORTATION AUTHORITY COLLECTION

OPPOSITE: The American Comet train, circa 1935. It was built in 1935 by the Goodyear-Zeppelin Corporation in Akron for the New York, New Haven, and Hartford Railway Company. The Comet reached 110.5 miles an hour on its test run. During its operation, it carried up to 160 passengers between Boston and Providence, a distance of 43.8 miles, with a stop at Back Bay Station in Boston, in forty-four minutes. COURTESY AKRON-SUMMIT COUNTY PUBLIC LIBRARY, GENERAL PHOTOGRAPH COLLECTION

BELOW RIGHT: Bain Ecarius "Shorty" Fulton with his vehicle, 1933. He was born in 1892 in Kenton, Ohio. He came to Akron in 1916 and was employed by Firestone and then Goodyear. In 1924, he bought a farm on Massillon Road, and, after clearing his pasture and orchard, began operating what was to become the Akron Municipal Airport. The airport was later renamed the Akron Fulton International Airport in his honor. COURTESY AKRON-SUMMIT COUNTY PUBLIC LIBRARY, SHORTY FULTON COLLECTION

BELOW: Pennsylvania Central Airlines plane at the Akron Municipal Airport, 1937. COURTESY AKRON-SUMMIT COUNTY PUBLIC LIBRARY, GENERAL PHOTOGRAPH COLLECTION

chapter five

MILITARY AND PUBLIC SERVICE

OPPOSITE: Men on the gondola of a TC Blimp at Goodyear's Wingfoot Lake in Suffield Township, circa 1923. The TC-3 and the TC-7 were US Army Corps non-rigid blimps used for parasite fighter trials. COURTESY AKRON-SUMMIT COUNTY PUBLIC LIBRARY, GENERAL PHOTOGRAPH COLLECTION

RIGHT: Akron City Council, 1880s. This meeting place in city hall was destroyed during the riot of 1900.
COURTESY SUMMIT COUNTY HISTORICAL SOCIETY, BUILDING SUMMIT COUNTY COLLECTION

BELOW RIGHT: Akron's electric police patrol, circa 1895.
COURTESY SUMMIT COUNTY HISTORICAL SOCIETY, CARL H. POCKRANDT COLLECTION

BELOW: Fire Station No. 2, engine and hose reel, circa 1885. The fire station was at Exchange and East Market Streets. Ollie Kintz, Gus Reinker, James Bunn, Levi Fox, and Charles Smith are included. COURTESY SUMMIT COUNTY HISTORICAL SOCIETY, CARL H. POCKRANDT COLLECTION

ABOVE: Spanish-American War soldiers marching in a parade, circa 1898. COURTESY SUMMIT COUNTY HISTORICAL SOCIETY, CARL H. POCKRANDT COLLECTION

LEFT: Akron Fire Department Engine House No. 2 (former Middlebury School), East Exchange and Market Streets, circa 1895. COURTESY SUMMIT COUNTY HISTORICAL SOCIETY

RIGHT: Ohio National Guard Fourth Regiment in front of the courthouse during the riot, August 1900. Officers, from left: Major Fred Titus, Lieutenant William Hunt, Captain Ed Andrews. COURTESY SUMMIT COUNTY HISTORICAL SOCIETY

OPPOSITE: Soldiers leaving Akron for the Spanish-American War, 1898. COURTESY SUMMIT COUNTY HISTORICAL SOCIETY, CARL H. POCKRANDT COLLECTION

BELOW RIGHT: Veterans marching on South Main Street in Akron on their way to Mount Hope Cemetery on Memorial Day, 1907. COURTESY SUMMIT COUNTY HISTORICAL SOCIETY, BUILDING SUMMIT COUNTY COLLECTION

BELOW: Postal workers in the Barberton post office, circa 1900. Included are Assistant Postmaster Robert Barnett, James Harter, Oliver Chisnell, William H. Davies, and Elijah Holderbaum. COURTESY SUMMIT COUNTY HISTORICAL SOCIETY

ABOVE: World War I enlistees with their friends and family at the intersection of Main and Howard Streets before leaving for the front, 1917. The Flatiron Building is on the left. COURTESY SUMMIT COUNTY HISTORICAL SOCIETY, CARL H. POCKRANDT COLLECTION

OPPOSITE: Soldiers leaving for World War I, 1917.
COURTESY SUMMIT COUNTY HISTORICAL SOCIETY, CARL H. POCKRANDT COLLECTION

LEFT: Postal workers in the Akron post office at the corner of East Market and High Streets, circa 1917. This building later became the Akron Art Museum.
COURTESY SUMMIT COUNTY HISTORICAL SOCIETY

LEFT: Akron Police Department, 1918.
COURTESY SUMMIT COUNTY HISTORICAL SOCIETY, CARL H. POCKRANDT COLLECTION

OPPOSITE: Policemen leading a parade, 1918. From left: Andrew Croghan, Jack Davis, Patsy Pappano, Adolph Oberdoerster, Marvin Galloway. COURTESY SUMMIT COUNTY HISTORICAL SOCIETY, CARL H. POCKRANDT COLLECTION

BELOW LEFT: Summit County Courthouse, circa 1918. COURTESY SUMMIT COUNTY HISTORICAL SOCIETY, CARL H. POCKRANDT COLLECTION

BELOW: Police officer sitting on a motorcycle outside Kenmore City Hall on Kenmore Boulevard in Kenmore, circa 1920. Founded in 1908, the village of Kenmore was built along the streetcar lines between Akron and Barberton. COURTESY AKRON-SUMMIT COUNTY PUBLIC LIBRARY, GENERAL PHOTOGRAPH COLLECTION

RIGHT: Akron Fire Station No. 2, circa 1920s.
COURTESY SUMMIT COUNTY HISTORICAL SOCIETY

OPPOSITE TOP: Akronites of the Ohio National Guard (Company L) getting a lecture on infantry tactics at Camp Perry, 1939.
COURTESY AKRON BEACON JOURNAL

OPPOSITE BOTTOM RIGHT: An 1888 model steam engine being pulled by two horses in the 125th Anniversary Parade in Cuyahoga Falls, September 30, 1937. COURTESY AKRON BEACON JOURNAL

OPPOSITE BOTTOM LEFT: Julius Greenfield, photographer for the *Akron Times-Press* testifying before the Senate Civil Liberties Committee, 1938. COURTESY LIBRARY OF CONGRESS / #LC-DIG-HEC-24836

BELOW RIGHT: Kenmore police standing beside the alcohol that was confiscated during a Prohibition raid, 1923.
COURTESY AKRON-SUMMIT COUNTY PUBLIC LIBRARY, GENERAL PHOTOGRAPH COLLECTION

BELOW: Man inside the USS *Akron's* control car, 1931. The control car, also known as the gondola, contained three rooms. The control wheels were located in the first room, the second room was used by the meteorologist, and the third room was occupied by the navigator.
COURTESY AKRON-SUMMIT COUNTY PUBLIC LIBRARY, GENERAL PHOTOGRAPH COLLECTION

chapter six

TRAGEDY

OPPOSITE: Large crowd gathering on Main Street to see the damage after the Crystal Restaurant collapsed on May 15, 1916. Nine people were killed and 30 were injured. COURTESY SUMMIT COUNTY HISTORICAL SOCIETY

RIGHT: Aftermath of the fire that destroyed Ferdinand Schumacher Jumbo Mill on Summit Street, March 1886.
COURTESY SUMMIT COUNTY HISTORICAL SOCIETY, CARL H. POCKRANDT COLLECTION

BELOW RIGHT: Ruins of the Schumacher Milling Company at Mill and Broadway after a fire, 1886. Five hours before daybreak on March 6, 1886, dust exploded in a grain-drying house among a group of buildings at Broadway and Mill Streets. The resulting inferno raged for two days and destroyed every building except the Empire Mill and a new office. Schumacher's loss was reported to be $600,000. Without insurance, Ferdinand Schumacher was forced to obtain bank financing to rebuild. He received this financing on the condition that his company be merged with the Akron Milling Company and that the new company participate in a trust that would fix prices and control the entire cereal industry. In 1886, Ferdinand Schumacher became president of the new $2,000,000 corporation, which immediately joined the 13-member Consolidated Oatmeal Company (the "trust") of Illinois. This association became the American Cereal Company in 1888 and Quaker Oats in 1901.
COURTESY SUMMIT COUNTY HISTORICAL SOCIETY, CARL H. POCKRANDT COLLECTION

ABOVE: Damage at the Akron Stoneware Company on Fountain Street after a tornado, May 10, 1890. COURTESY SUMMIT COUNTY HISTORICAL SOCIETY, BUILDING SUMMIT COUNTY COLLECTION

LEFT: Ruins of Frank J. Knapp's barn on Fountain Street after a tornado struck Akron on May 10, 1890. COURTESY SUMMIT COUNTY HISTORICAL SOCIETY, BUILDING SUMMIT COUNTY COLLECTION

ABOVE: Aftermath of a riot, 1900. The remains of City Hall are visible. COURTESY SUMMIT COUNTY HISTORICAL SOCIETY, CARL H. POCKRANDT COLLECTION

OPPOSITE: Buildings occupied by S. B. Lafferty's Bakery and Herrick & Son Store after collapsing due to faulty foundations, November 1891. COURTESY SUMMIT COUNTY HISTORICAL SOCIETY, BUILDING SUMMIT COUNTY COLLECTION

LEFT: View looking east from near the canal after the riot, 1900. COURTESY SUMMIT COUNTY HISTORICAL SOCIETY

RIGHT: Burning of the First Methodist Church on Broadway, 1911.
COURTESY SUMMIT COUNTY HISTORICAL SOCIETY, CARL H. POCKRANDT COLLECTION

OPPOSITE: The Cuyahoga River and Cuyahoga Falls during the flood of 1913. COURTESY SUMMIT COUNTY HISTORICAL SOCIETY, CARL H. POCKRANDT COLLECTION

BELOW RIGHT: Ruins near Case Avenue in East Akron after the flood, 1913. COURTESY SUMMIT COUNTY HISTORICAL SOCIETY, CARL H. POCKRANDT COLLECTION

BELOW: Crowd gathering to observe the ruins after the riot, August 1900. The riot began on August 22, when Akron police apprehended an African-American man named Louis Peck accused in the abduction and sexual assault of a local six-year-old girl. Outraged by the crime, a mob formed outside the City Building and demanded custody of Peck. When police refused to surrender the suspect, the mob became violent, exchanging gunfire with police, and hurling bricks and dynamite at the building. The violence escalated further as the crowd set fire to the City Building and adjacent Columbia Hall. Eventually, President William McKinley sent US troops to gain control of the situation and maintain peace. In the end, two small children were killed in the cross-fire, and Louis Peck was convicted and sent to a prison in southern Ohio. He received a full pardon in 1913. The riot remains the largest in the city's history. COURTESY SUMMIT COUNTY HISTORICAL SOCIETY

ABOVE: Onlookers observing firemen as they fight a blaze at the Pfarr & Hobart Co. hardware store at 990 East Market Street in Akron, 1915. COURTESY AKRON-SUMMIT COUNTY PUBLIC LIBRARY, GENERAL PHOTOGRAPH COLLECTION

OPPOSITE: People looking at the wreckage from an explosion of temporary school buildings in Barberton, June 1, 1939. On May 31, 1939, 58 people were injured, among them first- and second-grade children and school employees. The explosion occurred when gas that had seeped into the basement of the building from a broken line was ignited. The temporary school buildings, erected to house students while a new school was constructed nearby, were not in accordance with state laws regarding fire escapes, fireproofing, and the installation of gas detectors. Remarkably, no lives were lost in the explosion. COURTESY AKRON BEACON JOURNAL

LEFT: Wreck of the Mountain Line trolley in the Glens, Cuyahoga River Gorge, June 11, 1918. Four men were killed and two were injured. COURTESY SUMMIT COUNTY HISTORICAL SOCIETY

chapter seven

COMMUNITY

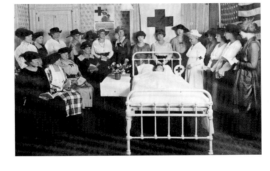

OPPOSITE: Achille Phillion performing his spiral tower show on Main Street, circa 1900. Phillion is also credited with bringing the first horseless carriage to Akron. COURTESY SUMMIT COUNTY HISTORICAL SOCIETY, CARL H. POCKRANDT COLLECTION

ABOVE: Sarah Gale with other ladies and children in front of her home on West Exchange Street in Akron, 1870. COURTESY SUMMIT COUNTY HISTORICAL SOCIETY, BUILDING SUMMIT COUNTY COLLECTION

RIGHT: The first electric light pole at Howard and Market Streets in Akron, 1880. It was 210 feet tall. People were told there would be so much light that farmers for miles around could throw away their lanterns.The experiment was a failure and the light pole was taken down. COURTESY SUMMIT COUNTY HISTORICAL SOCIETY

OPPOSITE: XX Century Camera Club, circa 1890. COURTESY SUMMIT COUNTY HISTORICAL SOCIETY, CARL H. POCKRANDT COLLECTION

RIGHT: Akron residents, circa 1900. COURTESY SUMMIT COUNTY HISTORICAL SOCIETY, BUILDING SUMMIT COUNTY COLLECTION

BELOW RIGHT: Early camera club, circa 1900. COURTESY SUMMIT COUNTY HISTORICAL SOCIETY, CARL H. POCKRANDT COLLECTION

BELOW: The Hudson Military Band, circa 1907. The band performed concerts in Hudson from the 1870s to the 1930s. COURTESY AKRON BEACON JOURNAL

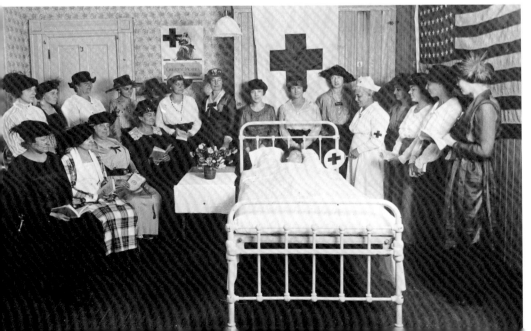

ABOVE: Great Western Band of Akron, circa 1910. Adam Ranck was the band's leader.
COURTESY AKRON BEACON JOURNAL

LEFT: Akron chapter of the American Red Cross participating in a class on home care for the sick, circa 1919. COURTESY LIBRARY OF CONGRESS / #LC-DIG-ANRC

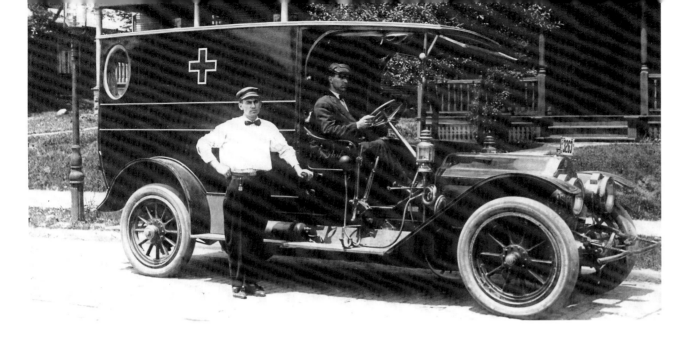

ABOVE RIGHT: Shorty Fulton with an unidentified man and three unidentified women from the Seiberling Beauty Contest, 1928. C. W. Seiberling was the co-founder and president of Goodyear. Bain Ecarius "Shorty" Fulton was born in 1892 in Kenton, Ohio. He came to Akron in 1916 and was employed by Firestone and later Goodyear. In 1924, he bought a farm on Massillon Road, and after clearing his pasture and orchard, began operating what was to become the Akron Municipal Airport. The land on and around Shorty's airport served multiple functions. When Goodyear began searching for land to build an airdock, Shorty suggested property next to his airfield. Goodyear accepted the idea. Shorty's airport also hosted motorcycle races, model plane meets, a skating rink, toboggan slide, ski jump, and the Soap Box Derby. In 1939, the Rubber Bowl was created from a depression left after dirt was taken to fill in a swamp area at the airport. COURTESY AKRON-SUMMIT COUNTY PUBLIC LIBRARY, SHORTY FULTON COLLECTION

ABOVE LEFT: Two men with a C. T. Parks Ambulance on South High Street in Akron, 1911. COURTESY SUMMIT COUNTY HISTORICAL SOCIETY, BUILDING SUMMIT COUNTY COLLECTION

OPPOSITE: Large crowd looking on as President Warren G. Harding's funeral train arrives at the Akron Depot, 1923. An Ohioan, Harding was elected as the 29th president of the United States. President Harding collapsed and died while in San Francisco midway through his first term. Harding had previously served as a United States senator from Ohio as well as Ohio lieutenant governor. COURTESY AKRON-SUMMIT COUNTY PUBLIC LIBRARY, GENERAL PHOTOGRAPH COLLECTION

LEFT: Administration Building of Akron City Hospital, late 1920s. The building was dedicated in 1904. COURTESYAKRON BEACON JOURNAL

RIGHT: Musicians at the City Mission in Akron, circa 1929. City Mission was founded in 1926 by Frank Wise and served the downtrodden in Akron until 1934. Frank Wise is in the far back, center. His wife, Louise, is also pictured, the third woman in the front row.
COURTESY AKRON-SUMMIT COUNTY PUBLIC LIBRARY, GENERAL PHOTOGRAPH COLLECTION

BELOW RIGHT: The American-British Choral Society from Akron, circa 1930.
COURTESY AKRON-SUMMIT COUNTY PUBLIC LIBRARY, GENERAL PHOTOGRAPH COLLECTION

BELOW: The tuberculosis clinic of Akron and Summit County at 326 Locust Street, circa 1929. Christmas Seal sales from 1922 funded the purchase of the centrally located clinic, which needed extensive renovation before it opened in early 1928. COURTESY AKRON BEACON JOURNAL

LEFT: Charles Knoske, Charles Sherbondy, Major Emmett Taggart, Alvin D. Miller, and Charles Dick speaking during the Memorial Day service at Glendale Cemetery, circa 1930. The speakers were the remaining members of the Grand Army of the Republic, Buckley Post 12. COURTESY AKRON BEACON JOURNAL

BELOW LEFT: The St. Peter's Church choir, circa 1930. Alfred Lee (center) served as choir director. St. Peter's Church was located in Firestone Park, a neighborhood in Akron. COURTESY AKRON-SUMMIT COUNTY PUBLIC LIBRARY, GENERAL PHOTOGRAPH COLLECTION

BELOW: Goodwill Industries truck used to collect donations, circa 1930. COURTESY AKRON BEACON JOURNAL

RIGHT: Helen Waterhouse (center), an *Akron Beacon Journal* reporter, interviewing Antonie Strassman (right), from Berlin, Germany, while waiting in a hangar at the Akron Municipal Airport, 1932. Strassman was one of Europe's most famous female pilots. In 1932, Strassman moved to the United States. She was later discovered to be a Nazi spy. COURTESY AKRON-SUMMIT COUNTY PUBLIC LIBRARY, SHORTY FULTON COLLECTION

OPPOSITE: William Falor (right), proxy of the student body at the University of Akron, and Hazabelle Davis (left), head of the Women's League, placing a wreath on the grave of John R. Buchtel in Glendale Cemetery, 1930s. John R. Buchtel was an American businessman and philanthropist, most famous for being the founding figure of Buchtel College, the predecessor of the University of Akron. COURTESY AKRON BEACON JOURNAL

BELOW: Commander Herbert Wiley, a survivor of the USS *Akron* crash, with four officers' wives, circa 1933. Mrs. Fay Brackett stands to the left of Wiley, and Mrs. Alger Dresel, wife of Commander Alger Herman Dresel (commander of the USS *Macon*), sits between two unidentified women. COURTESY AKRON-SUMMIT COUNTY PUBLIC LIBRARY, SHORTY FULTON COLLECTION

chapter eight

EDUCATION

OPPOSITE: Woodworking class at Bowen School, circa 1900. The school later became the downtown home of the Akron Board of Education.
COURTESY SUMMIT COUNTY HISTORICAL SOCIETY

ABOVE: Perkins Normal School students and faculty, late 1800s. The school was built in 1872 at the corner of Bowery and Exchange Streets at a cost of $10,000. COURTESY SUMMIT COUNTY HISTORICAL SOCIETY

ABOVE RIGHT: Akron High School's graduating class, 1883.
COURTESY SUMMIT COUNTY HISTORICAL SOCIETY

OPPOSITE: Akron High School football team, 1894.
COURTESY SUMMIT COUNTY HISTORICAL SOCIETY

RIGHT: Steels Corner School students, circa 1896.
COURTESY SUMMIT COUNTY HISTORICAL SOCIETY, CARL H. POCKRANDT COLLECTION

ABOVE: Members of the Lone Star Fraternity on an outing to Young's Sample Room (Young's Hotel & Restaurant), circa 1895. Lone Star Fraternity is the oldest local fraternity in the city. They were founded on February 22, 1882, at what became the University of Akron.
COURTESY AKRON BEACON JOURNAL

RIGHT: Akron Normal School's first graduating class, 1897.
COURTESY SUMMIT COUNTY HISTORICAL SOCIETY

LEFT: Akron High School's class of 1907. COURTESY AKRON BEACON JOURNAL

BELOW LEFT: Members of Akron High School's graduating class, 1896. Third row: George Gall (second from left), Walton Lyman (third from left), Anna Rampanelli (fourth from left), Wallace Foust (sixth from right), Gertude Tinker (fifth from right), Harrington Simpson (fourth from right), Charlie Akers (second from right). Fourth row: Gertude Mason (seventh from left). Fifth row: Lucille Pettey (third from left), Anna Bower (fifth from left), Blanche Hershey (sixth from left), Grace Cahill (seventh from left). COURTESY AKRON-SUMMIT COUNTY PUBLIC LIBRARY, GENERAL PHOTOGRAPH COLLECTION

BELOW: The basketball team at Buchtel College (later Akron University) after it beat Yale University 36-30, 1907. COURTESY AKRON BEACON JOURNAL

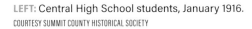

LEFT: Central High School students, January 1916.
COURTESY SUMMIT COUNTY HISTORICAL SOCIETY

OPPOSITE TOP: South High School football team, 1913.
COURTESY SUMMIT COUNTY HISTORICAL SOCIETY

OPPOSITE BOTTOM: Buchtel College's class of 1910.
COURTESY AKRON BEACON JOURNAL

BELOW LEFT: Class at the Maple Valley School at 1303 Copley Road in Akron, circa 1914. The school opened in 1914 and closed in 1929.
COURTESY AKRON BEACON JOURNAL

RIGHT: Tallmadge Grade School students, 1924.
COURTESY AKRON-SUMMIT COUNTY PUBLIC LIBRARY, GENERAL PHOTOGRAPH COLLECTION

OPPOSITE: The 1935-36 championship girls basketball team from Cuyahoga Falls High School. COURTESY SUMMIT COUNTY HISTORICAL SOCIETY, BUILDING SUMMIT COUNTY COLLECTION

BELOW RIGHT: Winners in the National Spelling Bee being received by President Calvin Coolidge, 1923. School children from all over the country who competed in the fourth annual National Spelling Bee held in Washington were received by President Coolidge at the White House. The winners are in the center of the group with the president. From left: Bessie Doig of Detroit, winner of the third award of $200; President Coolidge; Betty Robinson of South Bend, Indiana, the winner of the first prize of $1,000; Pauline Gray, representing Akron, winner of the second prize of $500. COURTESY LIBRARY OF CONGRESS / #LC-DIG-HEC-41332

chapter nine

RECREATION

OPPOSITE: Spectators watching Soap Box Derby racers cross the finish line at Derby Downs in Akron, 1938.
COURTESY AKRON-SUMMIT COUNTY PUBLIC LIBRARY, SHORTY FULTON COLLECTION

RIGHT: Men and women enjoying a meal at the Silver Lake Amusement Park dining room in Silver Lake, circa 1880. The Silver Lake dining room was located on the ground floor of the large dance pavilion. It had a table capacity for 500 people and was managed for many years by T. R. "Ray" McDonald, who later operated the Canteen Restaurant on State Route 8 in Cuyahoga Falls.
COURTESY AKRON-SUMMIT COUNTY PUBLIC LIBRARY, GENERAL PHOTOGRAPH COLLECTION

OPPOSITE: High Wheel bicyclists at Fountain Park, July 4, 1885. The Akron Bicycle Club members raced teams from other cities at Fountain Park. From the back, left to right, William Sawyer, Jay Steese, Walter Shields, Clarence Howland, Al Farrer, Charles Howland, Carl Sumner, Bert Work, Karl Pardee, Frank Kryder.
COURTESY SUMMIT COUNTY HISTORICAL SOCIETY, CARL H. POCKRANDT COLLECTION

BELOW: Men and women enjoying a rowboat ride at Silver Lake Amusement Park in Silver Lake, circa 1880.
COURTESY AKRON-SUMMIT COUNTY PUBLIC LIBRARY, GENERAL PHOTOGRAPH COLLECTION

RIGHT: High-wheel bicycle riders, circa 1890. John Kusch is fourth from left.
COURTESY SUMMIT COUNTY HISTORICAL SOCIETY, CARL H. POCKRANDT COLLECTION

BELOW RIGHT: Swimmers at Silver Lake Park, circa 1890. Second from the right is Louis B. Lodge, park founder Ralph Lodge's son.
COURTESY AKRON BEACON JOURNAL

ABOVE: The toboggan chute at Silver Lake Park, circa 1890. When it was first built, the chute was a rubberized, cloth-covered surface that was splashed with water before a rider's plunge; while the design helped make the ride a little smoother, it was still bumpy and caused swim costumes to rip. The chute went through many improvements in attempts to make the ride as comfortable as possible; one of the final modifications was giving riders actual toboggans in which to ride. COURTESY AKRON BEACON JOURNAL

LEFT: People gathering outside a vendor's tent at Silver Lake Park, circa 1890. COURTESY AKRON BEACON JOURNAL

LEFT: North End football team, 1898. Front row, from left: Burnette, Milo Williams, unidentified, Kromer. Second row: Cy Young, Kromer, Arthur Kauth, Jess McBurney, Otto Bedur. Third row: Fred Dietz, Theo Lantz, unidentified, Chas Hibbs, Roland Parker, Albert Schultz. COURTESY SUMMIT COUNTY HISTORICAL SOCIETY, BUILDING SUMMIT COUNTY COLLECTION

OPPOSITE: People enjoying a sunny day at Pleasant Park, 1898. Pleasant Park, a five-acre area, was dedicated as a public park in 1865 by Samuel Thornton when his 200-acre farm was annexed to the City. South High School was later built on the location of Thornton's orchard. COURTESY AKRON-SUMMIT COUNTY PUBLIC LIBRARY, ART WORK OF AKRON COLLECTION

BELOW: Baseball field and roller coasters at Silver Lake Amusement Park, circa 1900. The roller coaster at left was built for $12,000 and was 52 feet high and about 1,800 feet in length. It was a figure-eight, toboggan-style coaster. The tower and track were decorated with colored lights to attract visitors. The Racer at right was added later. COURTESY AKRON BEACON JOURNAL

ABOVE: The Akron Indians, 1908.
COURTESY SUMMIT COUNTY HISTORICAL SOCIETY, BUILDING SUMMIT COUNTY COLLECTION

OPPOSITE BOTTOM: Balloon race, circa 1916.
COURTESY SUMMIT COUNTY HISTORICAL SOCIETY, CARL H. POCKRANDT COLLECTION

LEFT: Men and bicycles line the front of Jacob Schwinn's shop, circa 1900. COURTESY SUMMIT COUNTY HISTORICAL SOCIETY, BUILDING SUMMIT COUNTY COLLECTION

TOP LEFT: Akron Indians football team, 1908. The Akron Indians date as far back as 1908. The early Indians teams won the Ohio League championships in 1908, 1909, 1913 and 1914. In 1916, The Akron Indians became the Akron Burkhardts (1916-1917), named for a local family of brewers that sponsored the team. In 1917, Vernon "Mac" McGinnis and Stephen "Suey" Welch bought the team and renamed it the Akron Pros (1917-1922). In 1920, the team changed hands and two local businessmen, Frank Nied and Art Ranney became the Akron Pros owners. Like many other semi-pro teams, Akron didn't play in 1918 because of World War I, but resumed action in 1919. In 1920, the Pros became a charter member of the new American Professional Football Association APFA. The new league didn't keep official standings, but owners voted in April 1921 to award the title to Akron on the basis of an undefeated record and only 7 points allowed in 9 games. The Pros had the first black coach in league history in 1921, when Fritz Pollard served as co-coach with Elgie Tobin. Pollard had been an All-American halfback at Brown University in 1916. Following winning the American Professional Football Association's championship in 1920, the team struggled. The Pros finished third in 1921 and tenth in 1922. The team only finished higher than thirteenth in the 1925 season, when it completed the season at fifth. Following the 1922 season, the Pros became the Akron Indians, an earlier Akron semi-pro team. This new team played for the next four seasons (1923-1926) before suspending operations in 1927 and surrendered its franchise the following year. In 2008, these early days of professional football were portrayed in the movie *Leatherheads* starring George Clooney, Renee Zellweger, and John Krasinski COURTESY SUMMIT COUNTY HISTORICAL SOCIETY, BUILDING SUMMIT COUNTY COLLECTION

OPPOSITE: Crowds watching a balloon ascending at the fairgrounds, circa 1920. COURTESY SUMMIT COUNTY HISTORICAL SOCIETY, CARL H. POCKRANDT COLLECTION

BOTTOM LEFT: Harness racing at the Summit County Fair, 1909. COURTESY SUMMIT COUNTY HISTORICAL SOCIETY

RIGHT: Crowd at Northampton Park watching the horse races, circa 1930. The racetrack was located on State Route 8 in Northampton Township. The name was changed to Ascot Park in 1938. After years of abandonment, the grandstands and other racetrack buildings were burned down as a firefighter training exercise in 1976. COURTESY AKRON BEACON JOURNAL

OPPOSITE TOP: Goodyear baseball team, 1930s. COURTESY SUMMIT COUNTY HISTORICAL SOCIETY

OPPOSITE BOTTOM RIGHT: Crowd gathering in front of the *Akron Evening Times* to "watch" Game 1 of the World Series, 1924. A man with a megaphone announced the play-by-play of the game, as figures moved around the diamond on the board. The New York Giants beat the Washington Senators 4-3, but the Senators won the World Series overall. COURTESY SUMMIT COUNTY HISTORICAL SOCIETY, CARL H. POCKRANDT COLLECTION

OPPOSITE BOTTOM LEFT: Samuel T. Daley and his saxophone band in Akron, circa 1930. COURTESY AKRON-SUMMIT COUNTY PUBLIC LIBRARY, GENERAL PHOTOGRAPH COLLECTION

BELOW RIGHT: The Goodyear Theatre players and orchestra from Akron, circa 1930. COURTESY AKRON-SUMMIT COUNTY PUBLIC LIBRARY, GENERAL PHOTOGRAPH COLLECTION

ABOVE: All-American Soap Box Derby, 1936. COURTESY SUMMIT COUNTY HISTORICAL SOCIETY

OPPOSITE: Sled riders at the Derby Downs in Akron, 1937.
COURTESY AKRON-SUMMIT COUNTY PUBLIC LIBRARY, SHORTY FULTON COLLECTION

RIGHT: Akron Yankees listening to their manager, Pip Koehler, before their inaugural training session, April 11, 1939. The Akron Yankees were a minor league baseball team that existed from 1935 until 1941. A class C farm team of the New York Yankees the club was based in Akron and played in the Middle Atlantic League.
COURTESY AKRON BEACON JOURNAL

chapter ten

CELEBRATIONS

OPPOSITE: Liberty Day parade on High Street, 1918. The structure at the left is the Gothic Building, which was still standing as of 2018.

COURTESY SUMMIT COUNTY HISTORICAL SOCIETY, CARL H. POCKRANDT COLLECTION

RIGHT: The Summit County Fair, 1880. It was held at Fountain Park, a 45-acre tract in the Little Cuyahoga Valley between North and Union Streets. The park hosted the fair into the 1920s. COURTESY SUMMIT COUNTY HISTORICAL SOCIETY, BUILDING SUMMIT COUNTY COLLECTION

OPPOSITE: The Knights of St. George marching in the Memorial Day Parade in Akron, 1897. COURTESY SUMMIT COUNTY HISTORICAL SOCIETY, BUILDING SUMMIT COUNTY COLLECTION

BELOW: Summit County Fair, circa 1900. COURTESY SUMMIT COUNTY HISTORICAL SOCIETY

ABOVE: The Walter Main Circus visiting Akron, circa 1900. The M. O'Neil & Company Dry Goods wagon was on site to sell to the gathering crowds. COURTESY SUMMIT COUNTY HISTORICAL SOCIETY, BUILDING SUMMIT COUNTY COLLECTION

RIGHT: The ballroom of Frank H. Mason's home on South Union Street decorated for a patriotic party at the turn of the century, circa 1900. Mason was a B. F. Goodrich executive, who later built an imposing residence at Turkeyfoot Lake. COURTESY SUMMIT COUNTY HISTORICAL SOCIETY, BUILDING SUMMIT COUNTY COLLECTION

RIGHT: Parade's drum corps, 1915. Fifers are Frank Fryberger and Ed Mustill. The drummers are Harvey E. Keefer and Ben Gintz. Harry D. Keefer is on the bass drum. COURTESY SUMMIT COUNTY HISTORICAL SOCIETY, BUILDING SUMMIT COUNTY COLLECTION

FAR RIGHT: Man holding two horses at the Summit County Fair, circa 1908. COURTESY SUMMIT COUNTY HISTORICAL SOCIETY, BUILDING SUMMIT COUNTY COLLECTION

OPPOSITE: Liberty Day parade on Main Street, 1917. COURTESY SUMMIT COUNTY HISTORICAL SOCIETY, CARL H. POCKRANDT COLLECTION

BELOW: Crowd gathering in front of Fred T. Child's Aeroplane Exhibit at the Summit County Fair, 1909. COURTESY SUMMIT COUNTY HISTORICAL SOCIETY

RIGHT: Parade on Main Street past the Flatiron Building, circa 1918. COURTESY SUMMIT COUNTY HISTORICAL SOCIETY, CARL H. POCKRANDT COLLECTION

BELOW RIGHT: Men, women, and children lining up with their horses and ponies for an event at the Summit County Fair, circa 1900. COURTESY SUMMIT COUNTY HISTORICAL SOCIETY, BUILDING SUMMIT COUNTY COLLECTION

ABOVE: Centennial Parade on High Street, 1925. COURTESY SUMMIT COUNTY HISTORICAL SOCIETY, CARL H. POCKRANDT COLLECTION

LEFT: Crowds of people along South Main Street, circa 1920. Visible along the parade route are Akron's Hippodrome Arcade, a dentist's office, J. P. Whitelaw (wholesale liquor dealer), and Osterman's Furniture. COURTESY SUMMIT COUNTY HISTORICAL SOCIETY, BUILDING SUMMIT COUNTY COLLECTION

ABOVE: A marching band in the Centennial Parade in Akron, 1925.
COURTESY AKRON-SUMMIT COUNTY PUBLIC LIBRARY, GENERAL PHOTOGRAPH COLLECTION

OPPOSITE: The Gough Lumber Company float in the Centennial Parade in Akron, 1925. In 1925, Akron celebrated the 100th anniversary of its founding with several days of festivities, including a parade featuring more than 4,000 floats, 7,000 marchers, and 23 bands. COURTESY AKRON-SUMMIT COUNTY PUBLIC LIBRARY, GENERAL PHOTOGRAPH COLLECTION

LEFT: Men marching in the Centennial Parade in Akron, 1925.
COURTESY AKRON-SUMMIT COUNTY PUBLIC LIBRARY, GENERAL PHOTOGRAPH COLLECTION

RIGHT: The formal pre-opening dinner held in the Mayflower Hotel in Akron, May 16, 1931. The 16-story, 450-room hotel was opened on May 18, 1931. It was built on the site of the YMCA building. The Mayflower became part of history in May 1935 when Bill Wilson, who was seeking help for his battle with alcoholism, made his famous phone call from the hotel lobby to a minister. This phone call led to Wilson's meeting with Dr. Robert Smith. Together they created Alcoholic Anonymous. In 1955, the hotel was bought by the Sheraton Hotel Company and the name was changed to the Sheraton-Mayflower Hotel, and eventually changed again to the Sheraton Hotel. In 1969, the hotel was purchased by Wellington Associates of New York who changed the name back to the Mayflower Hotel. The Mayflower Hotel closed on May 10, 1971. In 1973, it re-opened as the Mayflower Manor, a subsidized housing apartment complex.
COURTESY AKRON-SUMMIT COUNTY PUBLIC LIBRARY, GENERAL PHOTOGRAPH COLLECTION

OPPOSITE: Crowds gathering for the dedication of Goodyear's hangar, circa 1929. COURTESY SUMMIT COUNTY HISTORICAL SOCIETY, CARL H. POCKRANDT COLLECTION

BELOW RIGHT: Attendees at the Rubber Ball, 1938. The Rubber Ball was held at the Mayflower Hotel in Akron. C. W. Seiberling was the "King of the Ball" and Jeanette Verheyden was "Queen." Attendees had to wear costumes made of rubber. The event was idea of the Women's Art League.
COURTESY AKRON-SUMMIT COUNTY PUBLIC LIBRARY, GENERAL PHOTOGRAPH COLLECTION

INDEX

BUSINESS PROFILES

Brouse McDowell

In November 1918, with the end of World War I and a booming rubber industry in Akron, Ohio, two Summit County natives Edwin W. Brouse and C. Blake McDowell saw great opportunity and made a handshake agreement on Main Street in downtown to form a new law firm. This would eventually be known as Brouse McDowell, an Akron-based firm with more than 80 attorneys across five offices serving the needs of clients, the community and local area businesses.

They were soon joined by lawyers Amos H. Englebeck and Alexander H. Commins, and on January 9, 1919, the four men formally organized the firm Commins, Brouse, Englebeck and McDowell and established offices in the Central Savings and Trust Building at the corner of Main and Mill Streets. In 1931, the firm relocated to the Central Depositors Bank Building, later known as First National Tower, which remained the firm's headquarters for 73 years. Over the firm's history, it was given several different names through acquisitions of partners and mergers with other law firms, eventually settling on its current name, Brouse McDowell, in 1998.

As a staple in the downtown area, the firm has remained committed to philanthropy, service and community involvement. Attorneys and staff of Brouse McDowell give back to the local community, through participation in more than 150 professional, civic, cultural, educational and religious organizations. They volunteer their time through legal aid clinics to ensure equal access to high quality legal services and have served on numerous boards of non-profit organizations, including United Disability Services of Akron, United Way of Summit County, the Akron Community Foundation, and the Akron Children's Museum, to name a few. Further, the firm supports many local charitable causes, including annual sponsorship of the Akron Marathon to support the families served by Akron Children's Hospital, and in fact, was a founding sponsor of this event. The McDowell name is reflected at the Akron Summit County Public Library McDowell Branch, the Akron General McDowell Cancer Center, C. Blake McDowell, Jr. Galleries at the Akron Art Museum, and the C. Blake McDowell Law Center at The University of Akron School of Law.

Brouse McDowell has remained a downtown Akron business for more than 100 years, now occupying more than 60,000 square feet of Class A office space in the former B.F. Goodrich manufacturing complex, located at 388 South Main Street. The fundamental principles on which the firm was founded remain strong – an unwavering client service ethic and a strong commitment to service and community in the Greater Akron area. We are proud to contribute to the advancement of the legal profession and the communities in which we live and work, and we look forward to the next 100 years

BROUSE McDowell®
A Legal Professional Association
Celebrating 100 Years

Commins, Brouse, Englebeck and McDowell

Akron/Summit Convention & Visitors Bureau

Driving economic growth through visitor expenditures on accommodations, retail, dining and entertainment, the Akron/Summit Convention & Visitors Bureau (ASCVB) promotes Akron & Summit County as an ideal destination for meeting, business and recreational travel.

Established in 1973, the ASCVB is Greater Akron's award-winning destination marketing organization, having received 20 annual Top Destination Awards from the readers of Facilities & Destinations Magazine. Funded by a bed tax collected from visitors utilizing Akron/Summit County hotels, the ASCVB reinvests those dollars to develop and implement innovative and tactical sales and marketing initiatives. As the clearinghouse for the area's hospitality industry, information is compiled to ensure visitors, industry partners, community leaders/stakeholders are kept abreast of the area's vibrant cultural, entertainment and outdoor recreational offerings.

With an incredibly diverse array of travel and tourism offerings, Greater Akron boasts visitor activities and pursuits for all ages and interests. As travelers become increasingly savvier in deciding where and how to spend their leisure time and resources, the ASCVB continues to develop innovative ways to deliver information. Experiential themed attraction and event information allows individuals to focus their attention on what interests them the most, including: nature lovers, foodies/brewies (www.summitbrewpath.com), art enthusiasts, sports fans, power shopper and history buffs, to name a few. Additionally, information is available for several niche audiences: African-American, LGBTQ (www.outinakron.org) and Youth/Students. Providing current and comprehensive visitor information is the foundation upon which an exciting and memorable visitor experience is built. From printed guides to web sites and from social media outlets to personal consultations, visitors can expect current, in-depth and useful information. The ASCVB's annual visitors guide has received industry/peer awards from the Ohio Association of Convention & Visitors Bureaus and the Ohio Travel Association, while its web site placed 2 nd in a global contest sponsored by SiteFinity® . The ASCVB appreciates the accolades; but more importantly, the recognition underscores their efforts to produce and disseminate exceptional Greater Akron visitor materials.

Unique to only several Convention & Visitors Bureaus nationally, the ASCVB also manages and promotes the City of Akron-owned John S. Knight Convention Center and Greystone Hall. Spanning an entire downtown city block, the Center is the area's premier meeting, convention and exposition venue. Averaging more than 170 events annually, with attendance of nearly 400,000 guests, the Center compliments the ASCVB's efforts to attract business travel to Greater Akron by offering exhibit, convention and meeting services. To learn more about the positive economic impact the hospitality industry has on Greater Akron's economy and quality of life, please visit www.visitoreconomy.org.

With sights, sounds and special experiences awaiting you, take time to discover and explore Greater Akron and Summit County... this place we call home.

Akron/Summit Convention & Visitors Bureau
John S. Knight Center
77 E. Mill Street
Akron, Ohio 44308
www.akron.travel
www.playeatshop.org
www.johnsknightcenter.org
www.greystonehall.org
Email: information@visitakron-summit.org
800.245.4254

Stan Hywet Hall & Gardens

Historic Home of F.A. and Gertrude Seiberling

Stan Hywet Hall & Gardens is a National Historic Landmark that stands as a tribute to the Seiberling family and the early 20th Century era in which they lived. Synonymous with the tire and rubber industry, F.A. Seiberling was recognized nationally as the co-founder of first The Goodyear Tire & Rubber Company and later, the Seiberling Rubber Company.

Between 1912 and 1915, F.A. and his wife Gertrude built their American Country Estate. They selected the motto "Non Nobis Solum" meaning "Not for Us Alone," to represent their intentions for the new home. This belief continues to be embodied today as the estate is shared through education, tours, public programs and private events that welcome tens of thousands of visitors every season.

A 1937 Akron Beacon Journal article, stated, "One reason we all like the Seiberlings is because they never went 'high hat' on Akron; perhaps no other local family ever enjoyed greater prosperity and achievement . . . yet they were never so busy as to turn a disinterested ear to any pleader for Akron's future or civic welfare…"

The family used its fortune and influence to create fair housing, build a hospital, improve transportation both locally and nationally, preserve green space for the community's enjoyment and fund countless arts and culture programs and organizations. F.A. believed true prosperity was gained through the enlightenment and improvement of every citizen.

The Seiberlings' greatest legacy is in the homes, parks, businesses and organizations they funded or supported over one hundred years ago that like Stan Hywet, continue to impact Akron today.

Seiberling Heirs signing lease of property to Stan Hywet Hall Foundation in the Billiard Room, 1957.

Frank and Gertrude Seiberling.

Western Reserve Historical Society

Founded in 1867 as a historic branch of the Cleveland Library Association on Public Square in downtown Cleveland, the Western Reserve Historical Society (WRHS) shares the dynamic stories of Northeast Ohio and beyond – stories of the people, the artifacts and the archives that are the provenance for our region.

Operating six sites throughout Northeast Ohio, including Hale Farm & Village in Bath, Ohio. WRHS presents exhibitions, programs and experiences that tell the story of Cleveland and Northeast Ohio through art, documents and artifacts from a variety of collections at the Cleveland History Center in University Circle. It is through its vast collection visitors can learn about the history of Northeast Ohio, the innovation of those who lived here and how it can be transferred into modern economic expansion.

CLEVELAND HISTORY CENTER
of the WESTERN RESERVE HISTORICAL SOCIETY

From the very first map of Cleveland to LeBron James' championship shoes, journey through Cleveland's history from 1796 to today, with the extensive collection and interactive exhibits at the Cleveland History Center. Ride on the restored Euclid Beach Park Grand Carousel, walk through two historic mansions, experience the evolution of the automobile in Cleveland and the world in the Crawford Auto-Aviation Museum, and discover one of the largest costume and textiles collections in the United States. Cleveland Starts Here. Cleveland Starts with You!

hale farm & village
a museum of WESTERN RESERVE HISTORICAL SOCIETY

In 1810 Jonathan Hale purchased 500 acres from the Connecticut Land Company for land located in the Cuyahoga Valley. This portion of the country was referred to as the Western Reserve. In June, of that same year, Jonathan made the 646 mile trip to his family's new land and his wife and children followed shortly after. Over the course of the next 150 years three generations of Hale's lived on and worked the land, with an entrepreneurial spirit, in the Cuyahoga Valley.

In 1956 Clara Belle Richie, great granddaughter of Jonathan Hale, bequeathed the family's farm to the Western Reserve Historical Society. It was her wish that "Hale Farm is to be established as a museum so that the greatest number of persons might learn about the history and culture of the Western Reserve."

Over the course of the next 30 plus years Hale Farm has grown to become an experiential learning laboratory that creates a lifetime of social value.

Hale Farm & Village | 2686 Oak Hill Rd. Bath, Oh. | HaleFarm.org   **Cleveland History Center** | 10825 East Blvd. Cleveland, Oh. | WRHS.org

ABOVE: *The Akron Beacon Journal* was at Main and Bowery streets from 1906-1911. *The Beacon* has been proudly serving Akron and Summit County since 1839 COURTESY AKRON BEACON JOURNAL FILE PHOTO